THE AUTI

The Power is Within You

Gustavo G. Alcivar

THE AUTHENTIC MIND

The Power is Within You

Author: Gustavo G. Alcivar

Published by:
Kawsay International Development Group
429 Lenox Ave Suite 4C28
Miami Beach, FL 33139
Office: (305) 428-2576   Fax: (305) 393-8424
www.TheAuthenticMind.com

First Edition, 2008

Published in the United States of America

To my Love Celia, my Future Children, Parents, Brother and Sisters thank you for being present in my mind, heart, and life .

May all be well always.

Every human has four endowments; self-awareness, conscience, independent will and creative imagination. These give us the ultimate human freedom... The power to choose, to respond, to change.

- Stephen Covey

CONTENTS

The Authentic Mind

Introduction

The inner self can conquer the world with one finger if we allow ourselves to know that we can. Everybody else will state otherwise and we need to know how to listen to what our inner self is saying before the negative words of anybody else. How can we conquer this if turning the TV and watching the news, reading the newspaper, listening to the radio is telling us negative things? Children watching cartoon shows such as those that fight to save someone only gives the child of how to fight using his or her hands in a physical way. Ever wonder why a kid wants a sword or fighting figures for Christmas? We actually train our kids of the future to be part of the crowd when in reality we need to have them identify their inner self and be different than the rest.

We need to act now or we will continue to be part of a crowd on the road to nowhere and awaiting failures ahead. There are many good literatures such as the Power of Now and other similar books that teach us how not to procrastinate and fulfill our passion right away. Most of our retirees are retired from a position that they actually did not like doing, felt comfortable and maintained the status quo, or good incentives allowed them to stay there and fulfill their potential only to levels to achieve their job responsibilities. For those people I ask what about your remaining potential? Speaking from experience my mind would only go as far as routing aircrafts and technical skills. It took a challenge within me to realize I can do more than what my high school or college diploma states I can do. Now tell me who do you think was going to tell me what I am telling you now? Nobody from high school, college, boss from work would even dare to tell me my potential is farther than what my mind was trained to do. You are the driver of your State of Mind in pursuit of your inner self!

Elements of the Mind

In our mind we have imagination and adventures waiting to be unlocked and freed from fear of coming out. It's now when we need to act and not tomorrow or next week or next year as I sometimes hear. We leave things that will benefit us now for when we have time when in actuality time only exists in our mind. If somebody ever gives an excuse such as having no time I will always bring it back to the mind. You see the mind controls how we act or not act. The mind has us thinking every single negative thought of an action we are about to take when in actuality we can act first then think to avoid the delay. This allows us to do more and think later. This works for things we know will benefit us but at the moment we start to ponder about it and we steer away from actually doing it. Other things such as crossing the street obviously we need to think and make sure no cars are crossing before we act and actually cross the street, but for example deciding on starting a business why not do it and then think about strategizing. For example people will not form a corporation until all the strategy is in place, profit margins are set, and products are bought etc. but why not form the corporation and then do the rest. You will feel obligated to continue forward and the law of motivation will continue forward along with your passion. The idea is also to maintain yourself active enough on your passion that you will not have time to think about the negative thoughts that might appear if you wait before forming the corporation. I have many active corporations that were all formed before the idea was even born to give life to the corporation. I do not even think as I did before about where my next month's house payment will come from, I simply do not have time to think about it.

Nothing is a more common subject of remark than the changed condition of the world. There is a more extensive detail of thought, and a more powerful action of mind upon mind, than formerly known. The good and the wise of all nations are brought closer together and begin to exert a power, which though in an infant stage is felt throughout the globe. Thought is the force underlying all and what do we mean by this? Simply the following; your every act or every conscious act is preceded by a thought. Your dominating thoughts determine your dominating actions. In the realm of our own minds we have absolute control, or we should have, and if at any time we have not, then there is a method by which we can gain control, and in the realm of the mind become thorough masters. In order to get to the very foundation of the matter, let us look to this for a moment. For if thought is always parent to our acts, habits, character, life, then it is first necessary that we know fully how to control our thoughts.

The mind carries with it the power that perpetuates its own type of thought, the same as the body carries with it through the reflex nerve system the power which perpetuates and makes continually easier its own particular acts. Thus a simple effort to control one's thoughts, a simple setting about it, even if at first failure is the result, and even if for a time failure seems to be about the only result, will in time, bring the point of easy, full, and complete control. Each one, then, can grow the power of determining, controlling thought, and the power of determining what types of thought we shall and what types we shall not entertain. Thought is at the bottom of all progress, of all success or failure, of all that is desirable or undesirable in human life.

The type of thought we entertain both creates and draws conditions that crystallize about it, conditions exactly the same in nature as is the thought that gives them form. Thoughts are forces, and each creates of its kind, whether we realize it or not. The great law of the drawing power of the mind, which says that like creates like, and that like attracts like, is continually working in every human life, for it is one of the great immutable laws of the universe. For one to take time to see clearly the things he or she would attain to, and then to hold that ideal steadily and continually before the mind, never allowing faith — or positive thought-forces — to give way to or to be neutralized by doubts and fears, and then to set about doing each day what hands find to do, never complaining, but spending the time that he or she would otherwise spend in complaint in focusing thought-forces upon the ideal that the mind has built, will sooner or later bring about the full materialization of that for which is set out. There are those who, when they begin to grasp the fact that there is what we may term a "science of thought," who, when they begin to realize that through the instrumentality of our interior, spiritual, thought-forces we have the power of gradually molding the everyday conditions of life as we would have them, in their early enthusiasm are not able to see results as quickly as they expect and are apt to think, therefore, that after all there is not very much in that which has but newly come to their knowledge. We must remember, however, that in endeavoring to overcome an old habit or to grow a new habit, everything cannot be done all at once.

Unconsciously we are forming habits every moment of our lives. Some are habits of a desirable nature; some are those of a most undesirable nature. Some, though not so bad in themselves, are exceedingly bad in their cumulative effects, and cause us at times much loss, much pain and anguish, while their opposites would, on the contrary, bring as much peace and joy, as well as a continually increasing power. We have it within our power to determine at all times what types of habits shall take form in our lives? In other words, is habit-forming, character-building, a matter of mere chance, or we have it within our own control? "I will be what I will to be," can be said and should be said by every human soul. After this has been bravely and determinedly said, and not only said, but fully inwardly realized, something yet remains. Something remains to be said regarding the great law underlying habit-forming, character-building; for there is a simple, natural, and thoroughly scientific method that all should know. A method whereby old, undesirable, earth-binding habits can be broken, and new, desirable, heaven lifting habits can be acquired, a method whereby life in part or in its totality can be changed, provided one is sufficiently motivated to know and, knowing it, to apply the law.

Each one is so apt to think that one's own conditions, own trials or troubles or sorrows, or own struggles, as the case may be, are greater than those of the great mass of mankind, or possibly greater than those of any one else in the world. We forget that each one has his own abnormal trials or troubles or sorrows to bear, or struggles in habits to overcome, and that one is but the common lot of the entire human race. We are apt to make the mistake in this in that we see and feel keenly our own trials, or adverse conditions, or characteristics to be overcome, while those of others we do not see so clearly and hence we are apt to think that they are not at all equal to our own. Each has their own problems to work out. Each must work out their own problems. Each must grow the insight that will enable them to see what the causes are that have brought the unfavorable conditions into their life; each must grow the strength that will enable them to face these conditions, and to set into operation forces that will bring about a different set of conditions. We may be of aid to one another by way of suggestion, by way of bringing to one another knowledge of certain higher laws and forces, laws and forces that will make it easier to do that which we would do. The doing, however, must be done by each one for themselves. And so the way to get out of any conditioning we have got into, either knowingly or inadvertently, either intentionally or unintentionally is to take time to look the conditions squarely in the face, and to find the law whereby they have come about. And when we have discovered the law, the thing to do is not to rebel against it, not to resist it, but to go with it by working in harmony with it. If we work in harmony with it, it will work for our highest good, and will take us wherever we desire. If we oppose it, if we resist it, if we fail to work in harmony with it, it will eventually break us to pieces. The law is immutable in its workings. Go with it, and it brings all things our way; resist it, and it brings suffering, pain, loss, and desolation.

Thoughts and Character

In the degree that we attempt to use the thought-forces do we continually become able to use them more effectively. Progress is slow at first, more rapid as we proceed. Power grows by using, or, in other words, using brings a continually increasing power. This is governed by law the same as are all things in our lives, and all things in the universe about us. Every act and advancement made by the musician is in full accordance with law. No one commencing the study of music can, for example, sit down to the piano and play the piece of a master at the first effort. He must not conclude, however, nor does he conclude, that the piece of the master cannot be played by him, or, for that matter, by anyone. He begins to practice the piece. The law of the mind that we have already noticed comes to his aid, whereby his mind follows the music more readily, more rapidly, and more surely each succeeding time, and there also comes into operation and to his aid the law underlying the action of the reflex nerve system of the body, which we have also noticed, whereby his fingers co-ordinate their movements with the movements of his mind more readily, more rapidly, and more accurately each succeeding time; until by and by the time comes when that which he stumbles through at first, that in which there is no harmony, nothing but discord, finally reveals itself as the music of the master, the music that thrills and moves masses of men and women. So it is in the use of the thought-forces. It is the reiteration, the constant reiteration of the thought that grows the power of continually stronger thought-focusing, and that finally brings manifestation.

There is character build up not only for the young but for the old as well. And what a difference there is in elderly people! How many grow old gracefully, and how many grow old in ways of quite a different nature. There is a sweetness and charm that combine for attractiveness in old age the same as there is something that cannot be described by these words. Some grow continually more close to their friends and to the members of their immediate households, while others become possessed of the idea that their friends and the members of their households have less of a regard for them than they formerly had, and many times they are not far wrong. The one continually sees more in life to enjoy, the other sees continually less. The one becomes more dear and attractive to others, the other less so. And why is this? Through chance? - By no means.

Personally I do not believe there is any such thing as chance in the whole of human life, nor even in the world or the great universe in which we live. The one great law of cause and effect is absolute; and effect is always kindred to its own peculiar cause, although we may have at times to go back considerably farther than we are accustomed to in order to find the cause, the parent of this or that effect, or actualized, though not necessarily permanently actualized, condition.

It is well to find our purpose early, and if not early then late; but, late or early, the thing to do is to find it. While we are in life the one essential thing is to play our part bravely and well and to keep our active interest in all its varying phases, the same as it is well to be able to adapt ourselves always to changing conditions. It is by the winds of heaven blowing over it continually and keeping it in constant motion, or by its continual onward movement, that the water in the pool or stream is kept sweet and clear, for otherwise it would become stagnant and covered with slime.

If we are attractive or unattractive to ourselves and to others the cause lies in ourselves; this is true of all ages, and it is well for us, young or old, to recognize it. It is well, other things being equal; to adapt ourselves to those about us, but it is hardly fair for the old to think that all the adapting should be on the part of the young, with no kindred duty on their part. Many times old-age loses much of its attractiveness on account of a peculiar notion of this kind. The principle of reciprocity must hold in all ages in life, and whatever the age, if we fail to observe it, it results always sooner or later in our own undoing. In order to be concrete, even at the risk of being personal, I will say that in my own experience there have come at various times into my life circumstances and conditions that I gladly would have run from conditions that caused humiliation and shame and anguish of spirit. But invariably, as sufficient time has passed, I have been able to look back and see clearly the part that every experience of the type just mentioned had to play in my life. I have seen the lessons it were essential for me to learn; and the result is that now I would not drop a single one of these experiences from my life, humiliating and hard to bear as they were at the time; no, not for the world. And here is also a lesson I have learned: whatever conditions are in my life today that are not the easiest and most agreeable, and whatever conditions of this type all coming time may bring, I will take them just as they come, without complaint, without depression, and meet them in the wisest possible way; knowing that they are the best possible conditions that could be in my life at the time, or otherwise they would not be there; realizing the fact that, although I may not at the time see why they are in my life, although I may not see just what part they have to play, the time will come, and when it comes I will see it all, and thank God for every condition just as it came. The question is not, "What are the conditions in our lives?" but, "How do we meet the conditions that we find there?" And whatever the conditions are, it is unwise and profitless to look upon them, even if they are conditions that we would have otherwise, in the attitude of complaint, for complaint will bring depression, and depression will weaken and possibly even kill the spirit that would engender the power that would enable us to bring into our lives an entirely new set of conditions.

We are all in Life's great play— comedy and tragedy, smiles and tears, sunshine and shadow, summer and winter, and in time we take all parts. We must take our part, whatever it may be, at any given time, always bravely and with a keen appreciation of every opportunity, and a keen alertness at every turn as the play progresses. A good "entrance" and a good "exit" contribute strongly to the playing of a deservedly worthy role. We are not always able perhaps to choose just as we would the details of our entrance, but the manner of our playing and the manner of our exit we can all determine, and this no man, no power can deny us; this in every human life can be made indeed most glorious, however humble it may begin, or however humble it may remain or exalted it may become, according to conventional standards of judgment. We always blame the exterior world for all mistakes, delays, and circumstances in which I can state that the only person or world we should be blaming is ourselves and the world we created. We step into a world full of surprises that will bring us down to the ground, break our knees and assure us that we will never get up. So the story goes that education teaches us how to speak, think, learn, and analyze what we are given, but it doesn't tell us what to do to explore our passion and step out of that circle of influence that we all have. It is not a bad thing for each one to get a little "philosophy" into their life. It will be of much aid as one advances in life; it will many times be a source of great comfort, as well as of strength, in trying times and in later life. We may even, though gently perhaps, make sport of the one who has their little philosophy, but unless we have something similar the time will come when the very lack of it will deride us. It may be at times, though not necessarily, that the one who has it is not always so successful in affairs when it comes to purely money or business success, but it supplies many times a very real something in life that the one of money or business success only is starving for, though he doesn't know what the real lack is, and although he hasn't money enough in all the world to buy it did he know

Always remember that the great and strong character is the one who is ever ready to sacrifice the present pleasure for the future good. He who will thus follow his highest ideals as they present themselves to him day after day, year after year, will find himself eventually at the same gates. Life is not, we may say, for mere passing pleasure, but for the highest achievement that one can attain to, the noblest character that one can grow, and for the greatest service that one can render to all mankind. In this, however, we will find the highest pleasure, for in this the only real pleasure lies. He, who would find it by any short cuts, or by entering upon any other paths, will inevitably find that his last state is always worse than his first; and if he proceeds upon paths other than these he will find that he will never find real and lasting pleasure at all.

If at any time we are apt to think that our own life meaning is about the hardest there is, and if we are able at any time to persuade ourselves that we can find no one whose life is just a little harder than ours, let us not forget of those in countries currently at war or in need of financial help. Life can be defined and explained as a tree. For years it has been growing only "natural fruit." Not long since it was planted. The spring has come and gone. One-half of the trees were in bloom and the other half also. The blossoms on each part could not be distinguished by the casual observer. The blossoms have been followed by young fruit which hangs abundantly on the entire tree. There is but a slight difference in it now; but a few weeks later the difference in form, in size, in color, in flavor, in keeping qualities, will be so marked that no one can fail to tell them apart or have difficulty in choosing between them. One will be a small, somewhat hard and twisted, bitter, yellowish-green apple, and will keep but a few weeks into the fall of the year. The other will be a large, delicately flavored apple, rich, deep red in color, and will keep until the tree which bore it is in bloom again.

Why this incident from nature's garden? Up to a certain period in the fruit's growth, although the interior, forming qualities of the apples were slightly different from the beginning, there was but little to distinguish them. At a certain period in their growth, however, their different interior qualities began to externalize themselves so rapidly and so markedly that the two fruits became of such a vastly different type that, as we have seen, no one could hesitate in choosing between them. And knowing once the soul, the forming, the determining qualities of each, we can thereafter tell beforehand with a certainty that is quite absolute what the externalized product of each portion of the tree, will be.

If one would have a beautiful and attractive old age, he must begin it in youth and in middle life. If, however, he has neglected or failed in this, he can then wisely adapt himself to circumstances and give himself passionately to putting into operation all necessary counter-balancing forces and influences. Where there is life nothing is ever irretrievably lost, though the enjoyment of the higher good may be long delayed. But if one would have an especially beautiful and attractive old age he must begin it in early and in middle life, for there comes by and by a sort of collecting process when long-lived-in habits of thought begin to take unto themselves a strongly dominating power, and the thought habits of a lifetime begin to come to the surface.

Control of the Mind

Fear and worry, selfishness, grabbing, holding disposition, a moaning, fault-finding, irritating tendency, a slavery of thought and action to the thinking or to the opinions of others, a lacking of consideration, thought, and sympathy for others, a lack of charity for the thoughts, the motives, and the acts of others, a lack of knowledge of the powerful and inevitable building qualities of thought, as well as a lack of faith in the eternal goodness and love and power of the Source of our being, all combine in time to make the old age of those in whom they find life, that barren, cheerless, unwelcome something, unattractive or even repellent to itself as well as to others, that we not infrequently find, while their opposites, on the contrary, combine, and seem to be helped on by heavenly agencies, to bring about that cheerful, hopeful, helpful, beautified, and hallowed old age that is so welcome and so attractive both to itself and to all with whom it comes in contact. All types of thoughts, qualities, and dispositions, moreover, externalize themselves in the voice, in the peculiarly different ways in which they mark the face, in the stoop or lack of stoop in the form, as also in the healthy or unhealthy conditions of the mind and body, and their susceptibility to disorders and weaknesses of various kinds.

We are here for divine self-realization through experience. We progress in the degree that we manipulate wisely all things that enter into our lives, and that make the sum total of each one's life experience. We need to be brave and strong in the presence of each problem as it presents itself and make the best of all. Let us help the things we can help, and let us be not bothered or crippled by the things we cannot help. The great One of all is watching and manipulating these things in an intelligent manner and we need not fear or even have concern regarding them. To live to our highest in all things that pertain to us, to lend a hand as best we can to all others for this same end, to aid in righting the wrongs that cross our path by means of pointing the wrongdoer to a better way, and thus aiding him in becoming a power for good, to remain in nature always sweet and simple and humble, and therefore strong, to open ourselves fully and to keep ourselves as fit channels for the Divine Power to work through us, to open ourselves, and to keep our faces always to the light, to love all things and to stand in awe or fear of nothing save our own wrong-doing, to recognize the good lying at the heart of all things, waiting for expression all in its own good way and time—this will make our part in life's great and as yet not fully understood play truly glorious, and we need then stand in fear of nothing, life nor death, for death is life. Or rather, it is the quick transition to life in another form; the putting off of the old coat and the putting on of a new; the falling away of the material body and the taking of the soul to itself a new and finer body, better adapted to its needs and surroundings in another world of experience and growth and still greater divine self-realization; a going out with all that it has gained of this nature in this world, but with no possessions material; a passing not from light to darkness, but from light to light; a taking up of life in another from just where we leave it off here; an experience not to be shunned or dreaded or feared, but to be welcomed when it comes in its own good way and time. All life is from within out. This is something that cannot be reiterated too often. The springs of life are all from within. This being true, it would be well for us to give more time to the inner life than we are accustomed to give to it, especially in this world that we live. There is nothing that will bring us such abundant returns as to take a little time in quite each day of our lives.

We need this to get the kinks out of our minds, and thus out of our lives. We need this to form better the higher ideals of life. We need this in order to see clearly in mind the things upon which we would concentrate and focus the thought-forces. We need this in order to make continual progress and to keep our conscious connection with the infinite. We need this in order that the rush and hurry of our everyday life does not keep us away from the conscious realization of the fact that the spirit of Infinite life and power that is of all, working in and through all, the life of all, and the source of our power; and that outside of this we have no life and we have no power. To realize this fact fully, and to live in it consciously at all times, is to find Faith, which is essentially an inner kingdom, and can never be anything else. The kingdom of heaven is to be found only within, and this is done once for all, and in a manner in which it cannot otherwise be done, when we come into the conscious, living realization of the fact that in our real selves we are essentially one with the Divine life, and open ourselves continually so that this Divine life can speak to and manifest through us. In this way we come into the condition where we are continually walking with God. In this way the consciousness of God becomes a living reality in our lives; and in the degree in which it becomes a reality it brings us into the realization of continually increasing wisdom, insight, and power. This consciousness of God in the soul is the essence, indeed, the sum and substance, of all religion. This identifies religion with every act and every moment of everyday life. That which does not identify itself with every moment of every day and with every act of life is religion in name only and not in reality. This consciousness of God in the soul is the one thing uniformly taught by all the prophets, by all the inspired ones, by all the seers and mystics in the world's history, whatever the time, wherever the country, whatever the religion, whatever minor differences we may find in their lives and teachings. In regard to this they all agree; indeed, this is the essence of their teaching, as it has also been the secret of their power and the secret of their lasting influence.

In the highest education of the mind and life itself, such as we have been considering, there are those who feel they are handicapped by what we define as heredity. In a sense they are right; in another sense they are totally wrong. It is along the same lines as the thought which many before us had created in them through the saying: "In Adam's fall, we sinned all." Now, in the first place, it is rather hard to understand the justice of this. In the second place, it is rather hard to understand why it is true, and in the third place there is no truth in it at all. We are now dealing with the real essential self, and, however old Adam is, God is eternal. This means you; it means me; it means every human soul. When we fully realize this fact we see that heredity is a state of mind that can easily be broken. The life of everyone is in its own hands and one can make it in character, in attainment, in power, in divine self-realization, and hence in influence, exactly what he wills to make it. All things that one fondly dreams of are his, or may become so if he is truly in earnest; and as he rises more and more to his ideal, and grows in the strength and influence of his character, he becomes an example and an inspiration to all with whom he comes in contact; so that through him the weak and faltering are encouraged and strengthened; so that those of low ideals and of a low type of life instinctively and inevitably have their ideals raised, and the ideals of no one can be raised without its showing forth in his outer life. As he advances in his grasp upon and understanding of the power and potency of the thought-forces, one finds that many times through the process of mental suggestion one can be of tremendous aid to one who is weak and struggling, by sending him now and then, and by continually holding him in, the highest thought, in the thought of the highest strength, wisdom and love. The power of "suggestion," mental suggestion, is one that has tremendous possibilities for good if we will but study into it carefully, understand it fully, and use it rightly.

The one who takes sufficient time for himself or herself to form ideals, to make and to keep continually the conscious connection with the Infinite, the Divine life, and Forces, is the one who is best adapted to the difficult life. He who can go out and deal, with prudence and power, with whatever issues may arise in the affairs of everyday life. He who is building not for the years but for the centuries, not for time but for the eternities can go out knowing not whether he or she goes knowing that the Divine life within will never fail, but will lead on until one parts to the next life.

You are building for the centuries because only that which is the highest, the truest, the noblest, and best will abide the test of the centuries. You are building for eternity because when the transition we call death takes place, life, character, self-mastery, divine self-realization — the only things that the soul when stripped of everything else takes with it — has in abundance, in life, or when the time of the transition to another form of life comes, you are never afraid, never fearful, because you know and realize that behind you, within you, beyond you, is the Infinite wisdom and love; and in this you are eternally centered, and from it you can never be separated.

Use Your Mind Now

You cannot reasonably hope to succeed by dreaming about success even though it all starts with a dream or thought. You surely cannot achieve success if you go through your career living day after day in a repetitive atmosphere. You cannot really succeed without possessing some degree of personal magnetism. The growth of magnetism involves intense and continuous concentration of though upon a stronger field than our outer self. The value of magnetism consists in its practical application to everyday affairs. Success magnetism is not an accomplishment merely, it is a practical power. When rightly developed and used, it controls the subjective self in the concrete work of the objective. Magnetism is sanity at work; it is unalterably opposed to runaway fads, chimerical visions, unstrung nerves, and mental aberration. Magnetism is practical cooperation with level headed people who are bent on making the best of self and the world through created opportunity. That is why you cannot study magnetism too much nor practice it with so much faith. Its legitimate culture will not harm anybody and will benefit all who understand its synchronization with the mind.

Procrastination is so powerful that we give it a time a date of when we will do something and then reschedule it upon arriving at that date. We do this because it is in ourselves to go through life postponing the difficult matters and achieve the easy matter to feel good about accomplishing something. We do not realize that the difficult matters are the ones that allow us to grow and continue forward. We will notice that the difficult tasks will soon become easy and we should realize how to keep obtaining difficult taks if not we will head into a comfort zone and not grow. We can do everything our mind says we can do and the only reason we do not reach certain goals is because we tell ourselves "oh it's too difficult" I'll try again tomorrow. And we know how the story goes; tomorrow becomes a week and a week becomes next month, next year and so on. Ever hear someone say to you "oh just wait until you have kids and then you'll act responsible." That person is already telling you they waiting so many years to make changes and grow because their responsibilities grew. Why not act now and make sure your NOW is in the path to success. Don't be the one saying when I have kids I'll change. You will only be postponing your success until you have children and then you will still say you have no time because you have kids to take care of. The cycle keeps going until we decide to stop it.

We all have it in ourselves to do better than our parents and grandparents even if your parents or grandparents are wealthy. We have a thing called passion that is hidden in ourselves and doesn't find its way out unless we overcome the fear of fear itself. You see passion is a strong part of every successful woman or man's life. It allows us to explore or inner strengths with a purpose. Without it we are just normal beings following the crowd. We need to understand why passion is unique in ourselves and how not to be afraid to explore our inner self. Education takes us only half way to a life of success and happiness, the other half is within ourselves. Sometimes education is drilled in our minds as a necessity not realizing that sometimes you are the necessity to that college or institution and not the other way around. Don't get me wrong we all need education but after that diploma is handed to us there is nothing left except ourselves and student loans! If we all act now and realize that the now is more powerful than the past or the future we can all grow to what our passion is set for. Growth comes from within and part of growth is realizing what we have done up to NOW to be where we are. Only when you realize the decisions you took to be where you are you can then move forward to a better way of living. I call this relieving yourself from the past and starting up the engines for actions you take NOW. Put the past behind you and the future is on its way so just act and think about what you can do today. Tomorrow is not guaranteed and if tomorrow does come continue forward with even more momentum since God has given you another day. You might say I am healthy and tomorrow will come without a doubt, but I have read and heard stories of couples going to bed angry only to realize that the husband had a silent heart attack and tomorrow was gone forever for that person. We see how easily we can say that I wish I had gone to bed not being angry or saying I should had called my father the night before and say how much I appreciate their support from day one and express infinite love. We see the power that "today" has and the effects it will bring tomorrow.

A little less words and a lot more action guarantees our happiness and a peaceful mind. If we act as if today was our last day or if we absolutely know that today was our last day what would we do different I ask. What would be our priority and what would not be? Certain actions I took at a moment's notice have lured my direction in life. I can also say certain things I did not do I have suffered the consequences. I have only learned how to appreciate the moments and write this book to tell my story and give enough knowledge on the intentions of this book to make a difference now and not tomorrow.

We all know how to drive a car, but at first we needed to overcome the fear of not knowing what to do on the road. We took months to learn how to drive or to start driving on our own. We forget to realize that we overcame that fear and now we do not even think much while we are driving. We can do the same with our mind. We can train ourselves to overcome our greatest fear which is our inner self coming out with our passion. After a while you will not think twice about anything you wanted to do in life. You will do it and either conquer or fail but just like a car you can have the car break down or you can have a minor crash, but you will eventually get back on that road. You create a need to drive again to get from point A to point B. So why not realize that you are your own necessity and need to overcome any past fears and get up and go NOW! Not tomorrow or next year. Those New Year resolutions almost seems to have been created by people who want to wait until tomorrow or those who give themselves a set date of when they will get up and go. We all know what happens to those wonderful New Year resolutions!

We see how others have realized their goals and can state that while long hour days were sacrificed they are ultimate conquerors of their mind took advantage of now and not tomorrow. For example Walt Disney had the vision of what he wanted to do and did not waste one minute of his last years of life. It is said his last years were the busiest. It was as if he knew his time was short and needed to make sure his vision became a reality and protected for the future. Imagine if he said "oh I'm too old, I'll wait until the following year to start working on Disney Land and Disney World or I'll wait until I have more capital." No he took advantage even before ground was broken to have his vision gain momentum and ultimately have it become the well known children's world it is today. What would have been of Disney Land or Disney World if construction would have never been initiated? They say he didn't get to see Epcot or what Disney World is today, but he saw it first before anyone of us did. He experienced all the grand entrances, theme parks, new rides, expansion plans, parking locations, hotel space, attractions etc. in his mind before being built. We can now link having a vision and a purpose with giving life to our inner self. The passion to do something gives us that fuel that we need to live today with a purpose. Why not act like you are driving a car to a specific location in which you do not think twice about the fear of not knowing what to do. It's not the security of knowing if everything will be ok, but it's the passion and the way you use your Mind Now that matters most

You may be held where you are because you have no defined purpose in life, and if so, decide upon a purpose, proceeding at once to train all the forces of your being to work for that purpose and that alone. Gradually you will work away from your present environment and doors will open through which you may pass to better things. There is nothing that will take you into better environments more quickly than to have a fixed and high purpose and to marshal all the powers of mind and soul to work together for the promotion of that purpose. Since this is something that all can do, there is no reason for delays on why a person should live in surroundings that are inferior to himself or herself. You may also be held where you are because your good qualities are negative and have neither working capacity nor practical applications. If the better side of you is negative and if such tendencies as you may have inherited are positive and active, you are making for yourself a world that is anything but ideal. It is the worst in you that determines what kind of surroundings you are to receive, build up or attract. However, when your better side becomes strong and positive, when your good intentions are filled with living power, and when you turn all the forces of your being into the promotion of larger and higher aims, there is going to be a great change. In this connection one of the great essentials is that all the forces of your better nature be in harmony and trained to work together for those better environments that you have in view. Utilization of your Mind in the now or in the present is needed to accomplish all good things in your life.

Mind over Destiny

The destiny of every individual is determined by what he or she is and by what they do. What any individual is to be or do is determined by what he is living for, thinking for, or working for, be those objects great or small, superior or inferior. We are not being made by some outside force, nor is our fate the result of causes outside of ourselves. We are making ourselves as well as our futures with what we work for and in all efforts of following our ideals. It has been repeated in various languages, courses, and books that given the above then the following is true; he who lives, thinks and works for the superior becomes superior while he who works for less becomes less. Any individual may become more and create for himself or herself a better future and a greater destiny by beginning to think, live, and work for a superior group of ideals.

To have low ideals is to give the creative forces of the system something ordinary to work for. To have high ideals is to give those forces something extraordinary to work for. Our fate is the result of what those forces are constantly producing. Every force in the human system is producing something and that something will become part of both the individual and their external circumstances. Any individual can improve the power, the quality and the worth of his or her life by directing the forces of their system to produce something that has quality and worth. Those forces, however, are not directed or controlled entirely by the will, because it is their nature to produce what the mind desires, wants or needs. The desire of any mind is determined directly by the leading ideals entertained in that mind.

The forces of the system will begin to work for the superior when the mind begins to entertain superior ideals. Since it is the product of those creative forces that determine both the nature and the destiny of man or woman it is evident that a superior nature and a greater destiny may be secured by any individual who will accept and live up to the highest and the most perfect system of idealism that one can possibly comprehend.

To entertain superior ideals is to visualize in the mind and hold constantly before the mind the highest conceptions that can be formed of everything of which we may be conscious. To dwell mentally in those higher conceptions at all times is to cause the predominating ideals to become superior ideals since it is the ruling ideals for which we all live, think and work. It is not to dream of the impossible, but to enter into mental contact with those greater possibilities that we are not able to discern. To have the power to discern an ideal indicates that we have the power to realize that ideal. We do not become conscious of greater possibilities until we have developed sufficient capacity to work out those possibilities into practical tangible results.

To have superior ideals is not simply to desire some larger personal attainment, nor is it to dwell mentally in some belief of the world. To entertain superior ideals is simply to think the best thought about everything and to try to improve upon that thought every day. Superior idealism therefore is not mere dreaming of the great and beautiful. It is also the actual living in mental harmony with the very best we know in all things, in all persons, in all circumstances and in all expressions of life. To live in mental harmony with the best we can find anywhere is to create the best in our own mentalities and personalities. As we grow steadily into the likeness of that which we think of the most we will in this manner increase our power, capacity and worth, and in consequence be able to create a better future and a more worthy destiny.

To think of anything that is less than the best or to dwell mentally with the inferior is to neutralize the effect of those superior ideals that we have begun to attract. It is therefore absolutely necessary to think of superior ideals only, and to cease all recognition of inferiority or imperfection if we want to secure the best results along these lines. In this connection we find the reason why the majority fails to secure any tangible results from higher ideals, for the fact is they enjoy too many lower ideals at the same time. They may aim high, they may adore the best, they may desire perfection, they may live for the better and they may work for the greater, but they do not think their best thoughts about everything; therefore they fail to achieve higher ideals.

Superior idealism contains no thought that is less than the best, and it entertains no desire that has not greater worth in view. Such idealism does not recognize the power of evil in anything or in anybody. It may know that adverse conditions do exist, but it gives the matter no conscious thought. To pursue this course is absolutely necessary if we want to create a better future. For it is not possible to think the best thought about everything while the mind gives conscious attention to adversity and imperfection.

The true idealist therefore gives conscious recognition only to the power of good. The idealist lives in the conviction that all things in life are working together for the good. But this conviction is not mere sentiment with him because he knows that all things will work together for good when we recognize only the good, think only the good, desire only the good, expect only the good and live only for the good. To follow the superior ideal is to move towards the higher, the greater and the superior. No one can continue very long in the mode of living, thinking and acting without creating a new world, a better environment and a fairer destiny. We understand therefore that in order to create a better future we must begin now to select a better group of ideals for it is our ideals that constitute the cause of the future we expect to create. As the cause is so will be the effect.

Mind Building

To live is to move forward but there can be no forward movement without new experiences. Therefore in all advancement, in all progress, in all attainment, in all achievement, and in the living of life itself experience is indispensable. Experience being necessary to the promotion of advancement as well as to the increase of the value and the welfare of life, it becomes necessarily a permanent and continuous cause in the world of every individual, and as like causes produce like effects, both in quality and in quantity, experience should be sought and selected with the greatest possible care.

It is also highly important that we seek an abundance of experience because so long as the cause has quality it cannot be too extensive in quantity. Experience is the material from which character and mentality are constructed. Therefore the richer and more abundant our experience, the stronger and more perfect will our character and mentality become. Everything has its purpose and the real purpose of experience is to awaken new forces, new states, new phases of consciousness, and to originate new actions in the various parts of our lives.

The average mind makes no effort to select experience wisely, therefore fails to promote the real purpose of experience. Failing in this, one also fails to awaken and develop those things in life that can produce the most desirable of all experience, that is, the consciousness of a perpetual increase of all that has real worth in life. The more experience the better, provided it is rich, constructive and wholesome, though no person should seek experience for the mere sake of passing through experience. The belief that experience itself builds life is not true, nor is there any truth in the doctrine that all kinds of experience, good and otherwise, are necessary to the full development of life. It is only a certain kind of experience that can add to the welfare of life and promote the purpose of life. Therefore to understand the psychology of experience and how experience is connected with the workings of mind is a matter of exceptional importance. The daily purpose of each individual should be to seek the richest experience possible in order that the best material possible may be provided in the building of one's self. To this end one should place himself or herself in daily contact with the best that is moving in the world and the more of this the better. Such a practice will develop the mind, perfect the character, refine and re-polish the personality, and increase perpetually the health and the wholeness of the body. It will also tend directly towards the promotion of a long and happy life.

The mind should be wide awake to everything in its sphere of existence that can give expression to superior action, and seek to gain the richest possible experience by coming in contact with that action. To place one's self in mental contact with the best that is in action in the world is to originate similar actions within one's own mentality. These will arouse the superior forces that are latent in the deeper mentality and a long superior mental life will evolve.

The more experience that the mind can gain by coming in contact with the best things that are alive in the world the larger, the broader and the more perfect will the mind become. It is therefore evident that the loner must necessarily have a small mind whether he or she lives in the world or apart from the world. To live a life of seclusion is to eliminate experience to the smallest degree possible and thereby cause the mind to become so small that only a mere fraction of its power and intellect can be in conscious action. In consequence such a person can never be his or her best in anything, not even in a single isolated talent, nor can his or her ideas as a whole have any practical value, being based wholly upon one sided opinions.

The only intellectual satisfaction that is normal and that can be beneficial is that satisfaction which comes from the consciousness of continuous advancement. Any other satisfaction means mental inaction and leads to death invariably, not only in the intellectual but also in body, mind, and character. What is awakened in the mind of man is awakened by experience alone. For this reason no change in the mind can take place, unless preceded by some experience whether that experience be tangible or imaginary. What is awakened in the mind of man determines first what he or she is to think, and second what he or she is to do and be. This proves that experience is the material from which character and mentality are constructed.

Experience should receive the most thorough consideration during every period of life, and especially during the first twenty-four years of personal existence. The experience that a person passes through during this early period will determine to a great extent what is to be accomplished in later years, the reason being that the early tendencies are the strongest as a rule, be it good or otherwise. Do not get confused; man or woman can change his or her nature, character, mentality, habits, desires, or tendencies at any time. But time and energy can be put to better use in later life than to that of overcoming the results of mistakes that could have been avoided if the proper mental tendencies had been produced early in life.

To permit the young mind or any mind to pass through experiences that are unwholesome or adverse is to cause tendencies to be produced that will work against him all his life, that is, if those tendencies are not removed later on, and they usually are not. That person who enters the twenties in the consciousness of an abundance of rich experience is prepared for his or her career and will succeed from the very beginning. The person entering the twenties with no experience may be highly active but will accomplish little because being as yet unconscious of his or her real nature, real capacity, and true state of normal action will misdirect most of his or her energies and they will be used up before success begins.

The good things in the world should not be sought for mere pastime. They should invariably be sought for the purpose of gaining conscious possession of the richness which they may contain. This will increase immeasurably the enjoyment of the experience, and will cause the experience to add directly to the power, the quality, the worth and the value of life. It will make living more and more worthwhile, and nothing is worth more. The most valuable experience comes, not through mistakes, but through the mind's sympathetic contact with the best that is alive in the world. Such experiences, however, may not be obtained for nothing. A person who employs a small percentage of one's earnings in procuring such experiences is making a most excellent investment. The bank of rich and wholesome experience pays a very large interest. It will be profitable for everybody to deposit as much as can be spared every week in this great bank. To keep constant touch with the best that is living and moving in the world will give new ideas, new mental life, greater ambition, greater mental power, increased ability and capacity, and will in consequence increase the earning capacity of the individual. It will also increase the joy of living and make every individual life more worthwhile.

One of the greatest secrets of success in any undertaking, or in any vocation in life is found in the possession of a mental foundation so strong and so substantial that it is never disturbed under any circumstance. So it goes as the right kind of experience tends to build such a solid mental foundation, we realize the extreme value of the subject of Mind Building.

Mental Visualization

Every thought is patterned after the mental image that predominates at the time the thought is created. This is another great metaphysical law and its importance is found in the fact that thoughts are things, that every thought produces an effect on mind and body, and that the effect is always similar to the cause. According to these facts we can therefore produce any effect desired upon mind or body by producing the necessary though or mental state, so that when we have learned to control our thinking we can control practically everything else in life, because in the last analysis it is thinking that constitutes the one great cause in the life of the individual.

To control thinking, however, we must understand the process of thought creation. To think is to create thought, and to control thinking is to create any thought we like at any time and under any circumstance. When we analyze the process of thinking we find three factors involved, that is, the pattern, the mental substance and the creative energy. The pattern is always the deepest impression, the clearest image, or the predominating idea.

The quality of the mental substance improves with the quality of the mind, and the quantity increases with the expansion of consciousness, while the creative energies grow stronger the less energy we lose and the more we awaken the greater powers from within. When an idea or image is impressed upon the mind the mental energies will proceed to create thought just like that image and will continue while that image occupies a permanent position in consciousness. When the mind is very active a great deal of thought is created every second, though the amount varies with the activity of the mind. It is therefore more detrimental for an active mind to think a wrong thought than for a mind that is dull or less smart. This proves the fact that responsibility always increases as we rise in the scale. It is the function of the creative energies of the mind to create thought that is just like every image impressed upon mind and to continue to create thought in the likeness of that image while it lasts. The creative energies do this of their own accord and we cannot stop them. But we can make them weak or strong, or give them better patterns.

Mind is an art gallery of many pictures, but only the most prominent are selected for models in thought creation. Only those pictures that are sufficiently distinct to be seen by consciousness without special effort are brought before the creative energies as patterns. We thus find that the art of controlling one's thinking and the power to determine what kind of thought is to be created is acquired largely through the training of the mind to impress deeply only such mental pictures as are desired as models for thinking. The law, however, is very simple because as the picture in the mind happens to be at this moment so will also be the thoughts created at this moment, and the mental pictures are in each case the ideas and impressions that we permit in the mind.

Whatever enters the mind through the senses can impress the mind, and the result will be a picture or mental image which will become a pattern for the creative energies. What takes shape and form in your mind through your own interior thinking will also impress the mind and become an image or pattern. It is therefore possible through this law to determine what kind of thoughts you are to create by impressing your mind with your own ideas regardless of what environment may suggest to you through your senses. And it is by exercising this power that you place the destiny of body, mind and soul absolutely in your own hands.

As we proceed with this process we find another vital law which may be stated as follows: What we constantly picture upon the mind we shall eventually realize in actual life. This law may be spoken of as a twin sister to the one stated above as they are found to work together in almost every process of thought creation and thought expression. The one declares that all thought is patterned after the predominating mental pictures while the other declares that the entire external life of man or woman is being daily recreated in the likeness of those mental pictures. The fact is, as the mental tendencies are, so is thought; as thought is, so is character; and it is combined action of character, ability and purpose that determines what we are to attain or accomplish, or what is to happen to us.

Through the law of attraction we naturally meet in the external world what corresponds to our own internal world, that is, to what we are in ourselves. The self constitutes the attraction, and like attracts like. This self which constitutes the attraction is composed of all the active forces, desires, tendencies, motives, states and thoughts that are at work in mind or personality. When we look at everything that is alive throughout our whole being and put all those things together we have what may be defined as our present active self. This self invariably attracts in the external world such conditions as corresponds to its own nature. This self and all its parts in the person correspond to the thoughts that we have been creating in mind. In fact the nature of the self is actually composed of thought, mental states and mental activities. We realize, therefore, that when we change our thought, the nature of the self will change, and this change will be good or otherwise depending upon the change of thought.

Your external life is the exact counterpart of this active self. This self is the exact likeness of your thought, and your thoughts are patterned after the images that are impressed upon your mind. Therefore we understand that whatever is pictured in the mind will be realized in external life and the reason why is not only simply explained but can be proven along strictly scientific lines. However, to determine through the law of mind visualization what our external life is to be, every process of mind visualization which we desire to carry out must be continued for a sufficient length of time to give the creative processes the opportunity to make over the whole self.

When a certain image is formed in the mind thought will be created in the likeness of that image. This thought goes out and permeates the entire self and changes the self to a degree. But as a rule it takes some time to change the entire self; therefore we must continue to hold the desired visualizations in mind until the whole self has been entirely made over and has become just like the ideal image. You can easily discern when the self has been wholly changed because as soon as the self is changed everything in your life changes. Then a new self will attract new people, new conditions, new environments, new opportunities and new states of being. It is evident therefore that so long as there is no change in the outer life we may know that the self has not been changed. However, the changing process may be going on, but the new has yet become stronger than the old, and for the time being things continue as they were.

When the self has been changed to such an extent that the new becomes positive and the old negative we will begin to attract new things. We may therefore begin to attract new and better things for some time before the entire self has been completely changed. When we are changing only a part of the self that part will begin to attract the new while those parts of the self that have not been changed will continue to attract the old as usual. This explains why some people continue to attract trouble and adversity for a while after they have begun to live a larger and a better life.

In promoting the art of mind visualization we must not change ideas or plans at too frequent intervals for such changes will neutralize what has been gained thus far and here is the place where many people fail. The average person who wishes to change his or her life for the better does not hold on to his or her ideals long enough; that is, he or she does not give them a fair chance to work themselves out and bring the expected results. When one does not receive results as soon as one expects it then one has to change the plans and produce new pictures upon the mind. When our ideals are the highest we know we do not have to change them. They cannot be improved upon until we have so entirely recreated ourselves that we can live in a superior state of consciousness. It is therefore highly important to determine positively upon the ideals that we wish to realize, and to hold on to those ideals until they are realized regardless of what may happen in the meantime.

To be realized means that a mental image must be constant, but only such visualization can be constant as are sufficiently elaborate to involve a complete transformation in yourself, and that are so high that they can act as an inspiration until all your present ideals are realized. When we form such visualizations in the mind and continue to hold on to them until they are externally realized we shall certainly obtain the desired realization. At such times we can proceed with the perfect faith that what we have visualized will become true in actual life in days to come, and those days will not be far away. But to use this law the mind must never divert; it must hitch its route to a star and never cut the traces.

In scientific mind visualization it is not necessary to go into minor details, though we must not be too general.

The idea is to picture all the essentials, that is, all those parts that are distinct or individualized. But we need not include such things as are naturally attracted by the essentials. In other words, apply the law, and that which will naturally come through the application of the law, will be realized.

If you wish to realize a more perfect body it is not necessary to picture the exact physical appearance of that body. You may not know at present what a perfect body should look like. Therefore visualize only the quality of perfection in every part of the physical form and those qualities will develop and express themselves more and more throughout your personality.

If you wish to enter a different environment do not give your thought to some special locality, nor to persons and things that would necessarily be included in such an environment. Persons come and go and things are generally the way we wish them to be. To proceed realize what constitutes an ideal environment and hold that picture in your mind. In analyzing an ideal environment we would find it to contain harmony, beauty, love, peace, joy, desirable opportunities, advantages, ideal friends, wholesome conditions and an abundance of the best of everything that the welfare of human life may require. Therefore we should picture those things and continue to hold them in mind with the faith that we will soon find an environment containing all those things in the highest degree of perfection. Gradually we shall find more and more of them coming into our life until we shall find an environment that comes up in every respect to our ideal.

The law of mind visualization will also be found effective in changing physical conditions. Any physical problem must eventually disappear if we continue to hold in mind a perfect picture of health and wholeness. Many have eliminated chronic ailments in a few weeks and even in a few days by this method, and all would succeed if they never pictured disease but perfect health only. In the field of achievement we will find the same facts to be true. Whenever we fear that we shall not succeed we bring forth the wrong picture, thus the wrong thoughts are created and wrong conditions are produced; in consequence the very thing we feared comes upon us. When we are positively determined to succeed, however, we picture the idea of success and attainment upon the mind, and according to the law, success will be realized in external life.

Mental and spiritual attainments respond remarkably to mind picturing, principally because all true mind picturing draws consciousness up into the world of superiority. The same is true in the field of talent. If there is any talent that you wish to develop, draw mental pictures of yourself in full possession of that talent and you will comply with the requirements of the steady growth of that talent. This method alone will accomplish much, but when it is associated with our processes of development the results desired will surely be remarkable. It is the way we think that determines the quality of the mind, and it is the quality of the mind that determines what our ability, mental capacity and mental force is to be. We can readily understand that the improvement of ability will naturally be followed by increase in attainment and achievement as well as a greater control over fate and destiny. Man and woman are constantly increasing their ability, making their own future and making that future brighter and greater every day. Therefore, if mind pictures can affect mental quality, mental power and mental ability they can also affect environment and achievement, and in brief, the entire external life of man. In looking for evidence for the fact that mental pictures can affect ability, simply compare results from efforts that are inspired by high ideals and efforts that are inspired by low ideals and you have all the evidence you need. When your mind is filled with pictures of superiority you will think superior thoughts, thoughts that have more quality, power and worth, and such thoughts cannot fail to give power, quality and worth to your talents and faculties. We also find that tendencies, desires and motives originate largely from mental pictures, and we also know that these factors exercise an enormous power in life. The active self of man and woman are so dominated by desires and tendencies that it is absolutely impossible to change the self until tendencies and desires are changed. But tendencies and desires as well as motives cannot be changed without changing the mental pictures.

The mind is very large. It is therefore possible to form mental pictures of as many ideals as we like, but at first it is best to choose only a few. Begin by picturing a perfect body, an able mind, a strong character and a beautiful soul; after that an ideal interior life and an ideal external environment. Thus you have the foundation of a great, rich and wonderful life. Keep these pictures constantly before your mind; in fact train yourself to actually live for those pictures. You will find all things in your life changing daily to become more and more like those pictures. In the course of time you will realize in actual life the exact likeness of those pictures; that is, what you have constantly pictured upon your mind you will realize in actual life. Then you can form new and more beautiful pictures to be realized in like manner as you build for a still greater future.

Mind over Body

It is through the law of vibration that the mind exercises its power over the body. And through this law every action of the mind produces a chemical effect in the body, that is, an effect that actually takes place in the substance of the physical form. The process of this law is readily understood when we find that every mental action is a vibration, and passes through every atom in the body, modifying both the general conditions and the chemical conditions of every group of cells.

A chemical change in the body is produced by a change in the vibrations of the different elements of the body because every element is what it is by virtue of the rate of vibrations of its atoms. Everything in the universe is what it is because of its rate of vibration; therefore, anything may be changed in nature and quality by changing the rate of its vibrations. When we change the vibration of ice it becomes water. When we change the vibrations of water it becomes steam. When we change the vibrations of ordinary earth in one or more ways it becomes green grass, roses, trees or waving fields of grain, depending upon the changes that are made. Nature is constantly changing the vibrations of her elements thus producing all sorts of forms, colors and appearances. In fact, the vast panorama of nature, both that which is visible to the senses and that which is not all is produced by constant changes in the vibrations of the elements and forces of nature.

Human beings, however, is doing the same in his or her kingdom, that is, in mind and personality. We all are changing the vibrations of different parts of our system every second, though all such changes are, of course, produced within the bounds of natural law. We know that by exercising the power of thought in any form or manner we can produce the vibrations both of our state of mind and our physical conditions. When we exercise this power to the fullest degree possible we can change the vibrations of everything in our system and thus produce practically any condition that may be desired.

This gives us a power that is extraordinary to say the least. But it is not a power that we have to secure. We have it already and we employ it every minute, because to think is to exercise this power. This being true the problem is to use this power intelligently and thus not only secure desirable results, or results as desired, but also to secure superior results to anything we have secured before.

When we analyze this law of vibration we find that every unpleasant condition that man has felt in his or her body has come from a false change in the vibrations of some of the elements of the body. We also find that every agreeable condition has come from a true change in those vibrations, that is, a change towards the better. Here we should remember that every change in the vibrations of the human system that takes us down, so to speak into the lesser grade is a false change and will produce unnatural or detrimental effects, while every change that is an ascending change in the scale is beneficial. To apply this law intelligently it is necessary to know what chemical changes each particular mental action has the power to produce, and also how we may so regulate mental actions that all changes in the vibrations of our system may be changes along the line of the ascending scale. This, however, leads us into a vast and most fascinating subject; but on account of its vastness we can only mention it here, which is all that is necessary in this connection, as our object for the present is simply to give the reason why every mental action produces a chemical change in the body.

Since every element in the body is what it is because it vibrates at a certain rate; since every mental action is a vibration; since every vibration that comes from an inner plane can modify vibrations that act upon an outer plane; and since all vibrations are within the physical plane of action, we understand perfectly why every mental action will tend to produce a chemical change in the body. Although it is also true that two different grades of vibration on the same plane, or in the same sphere of action, may modify each other, still they do so only when the one is much stronger than the other.

All mental vibrations act more deeply in chemical life than the physical vibrations; therefore the former can entirely change the latter, no matter how strong the latter may seem to be. And this is how the mind exercises power over the body. Some mental vibrations, however, are almost as near to the surface as the physical ones and for that reason produce but slight changes, changes that are sometimes imperceptible. Knowing this we understand why the power of mind over body becomes greater in proportion to the depth of consciousness and feeling that we enter into during any process of thought. Therefore when we promote such changes in the body as we may desire or decide upon we must cultivate deeper consciousness, or what may be called subjective consciousness.

This is extremely important because we can eliminate practically any physical disease or undesired physical condition by producing the necessary chemical change in those physical elements where that particular condition resides at the time. This is how medicine aims to cure and it does cure whenever it produces the necessary chemical change. But it fails so frequently in this respect that it cannot be depended upon under all circumstances.

Mental vibrations, however, when deep or subjective can in every case produce the necessary chemical change in the elements concerned, and the desired vibrations are invariably produced by positive, constructive and wholesome mental actions, provided those actions are deeply felt. Thus we realize that the power of mind acting through the law of vibrations can, by changing or modifying the vibrations of the different elements in the body, produce almost any change desired in the physical conditions of the body.

What we wish to emphasize in this connection are the facts that every mental action is a vibration; that it permeates every atom of the body; that it comes up from the deeper chemical life, thereby working beneath the elements and forces of the physical body; and that according to a chemical law can modify and change the vibrations of those elements and forces to almost any extent within the sphere of natural law. To modify the vibrations of the physical elements is to produce a chemical change in the body. But whether this change will be desirable or undesirable depends upon the nature of the mental action that produces the change. Therefore by entertaining and perpetuating only such mental actions as tend to produce desirable changes, or the changes we want in the body, we can secure practically any physical change desired; and we may thereby exercise the power of mind over body to an extent that will have practically no limitations within the natural workings of the human domain.

Growth of the Mind

All mental actions that consciously move towards the within tend to increase the capacity, the power and the quality of mind. The majority of mental actions in the average mind, however, move towards the surface, and this is one reason why advancing years bring mental inferiority as the converse of this law is also true. That is, that all mental actions that move towards the surface will decrease the power of mind.

According to the law of growth the more we use the mind, the larger and stronger and more perfect it should become, provided it is used properly. Therefore continuous use in itself should invariably bring increase. However, the use of anything may follow the lines of destruction as well as construction. For this reason we must train all mental actions along constructive lines. And we find all constructive actions tends to deepen mental action; in other words, tends to move towards the within.

The value of the increase of mental power is clearly evident along all lines. Everything must increase in the life of him or her who is perpetually increasing his or her own personal power. We know that a large mind creates more extensively than a small one. The creations of a highly developed mind are more worthy than the creations of an inferior mind, and the achievements of any one are in proportion to that one's capacity and power. Therefore when we begin to increase the value of life everything pertaining to life as well as everything coming into life will increase also. Perpetual development in us means perpetual increase of everything of worth required in our sphere of existence. This is the law; but so long as mental actions move towards the surface, mentality is diminished; therefore the opposite process must be established.

By training all mental actions to move constantly towards the within we increase perpetually the capacity, the power and the quality of mind and the reason why is very simple. When mental actions move towards the surface, consciousness will be centered upon the surface of things and will therefore picture in mind the lesser and inferior side of things. Those mental energies that serve as patterns for the creative energies will in consequence be formed in the likeness of the smaller. And the result is that the mind will be created according to the lesser and more inferior conception of itself.

On the other hand, when all the actions of mind move toward the great within, the eye of the mind will concentrate upon the world of greater possibilities. The conception of things will in such a mental state constantly increase because attention at such times is concerned only with that which is larger and superior. Thus the mental energies will be directed towards the idea of superiority, and the creative energies will naturally rebuild the mind gradually and steadily upon a larger and more perfect scale. This is all very simple and anyone who will examine the workings of his own mind will find it to be absolutely true. We understand therefore how each individual has in his or her own hands the power to create for themselves a greater mind, a more perfect personality, a richer life and a more desirable destiny.

In all methods for mental development this law must be wisely considered for no matter how perfect the method may be, if the mental actions move towards the surface, no results will be gained. While on the other hand, if the mental actions move towards the within results will positively be gained even though the methods be inferior. Nearly all minds in the past that continued to develop through life did so without system, but gained increase through aspiration, or rather concentration upon the greater possibilities of life, which in turn caused mental actions to move towards the within.

When your attention is turned upon the inner and the larger phases of life your mind will begin to turn its actions upon the great within. Accordingly all mental tendencies will begin to move toward superiority, and all the building forces in your life will have superiority as their goal. That you should constantly rise in the scale when thinking and acting in this manner is therefore evident. Remarkable results have been gained and can be gained simply through aspiration, but if a complete system of the best methods is employed in conjunction with the fundamental law, these results will naturally increase to a very great degree. For this reason all things that are conducive to the growth of the mind should be employed in harmony so that the increase of mental power may be gained in the largest possible measure.

To train the mental actions to move towards the within we should concentrate attention upon the greater possibilities of life, and think as deeply and as much as we can upon those possibilities. In fact we should train the mind to look towards the within at all times and view with great expectations those superior states that long will be attained. In addition all tendencies of life should be trained to move towards the higher and the larger and every thought should have an ascending spirit.

When you feel that you are becoming too much concerned with the superficial, turn attention at once upon the depths of existence. And when you feel that you have fallen down temporarily into the world of inferiority use every effort at your command to rise again. The leading purpose should be to train all the forces, desires, tendencies and actions in life to move upward and onward at all times. This will cause the greater powers and possibilities within to be awakened, which will be followed by the perpetual increase of the capacity, the power and the quality of the mind. And with this increase comes also the increase of everything else in life that is required for our highest welfare.

When this increase of power begins it will naturally be felt in various parts of mind, and in order to know how to make the best possible use of this increase, as well as of the power we already possess, we should remember the great law, that whatever you feel that you can do, that you have the power to do. There are many methods through which we can determined what the mind really can do and what work we may be able to carry out successfully, but this particular law is the best guide of all, provided it is properly understood. And it is extremely important to discover what we are able to do because the majority is not in their true spheres of action. To be in your true sphere of action means better work, greater results and more abundant good both to yourself and to others with whom you are associated. It also means that you can be at your best at all times and he who is at his best at all times is on the way to perpetual growth and perpetual increase.

To do your best work and your true work you must employ the largest and the strongest ability that you possess. But to learn what this ability actually is, this is the problem. This problem can be solved, however, if we live in compliance with the law just mentioned. The power that we possess is always felt; therefore when you feel that you can do a certain thing it means that there is sufficient power in that particular ability that is required. But ability must be large before it can contain enough power to be consciously felt. Consequently the fact that you feel power in a certain ability proves conclusively that the ability is large and is possessed of considerable power. From this point on, the question to decide is, where you feel the greatest amount of power because where you feel the most power there you will find the greatest ability. This is conclusive, but here another question arises, that is, if the feeling of the average person is always reliable. The answer is that it is not.

But it can be made so with a little training. All psychologists have come to the conclusion that there is but one sense, the sense of feeling and that all other senses, both in the external and the internal are but modifications of this one sense. It is also admitted that the sense of feeling can be cultivated along scores of lines where it is now entirely inactive, and that there is no perceptible limit to its development along any line. This being true we shall go to the very foundation of all the senses, and all the modes of discerning things, when we take the senses of feeling for our guide in the selection of that work for which we have the greatest talent and power.

To train the sense of feeling in detecting the exact place in mind where the greatest power resides, the first step is to make this sense normal, which is highly important because the average person has so many artificial desires, and permits the mind to be stimulated by every successful venture that is heard of. There are a many people who become aroused with ambition to enter the entrepreneurial world whenever they learn of remarkable success attained in that world. Thus their energies are temporarily turned upon the entrepreneurial faculties and they feel considerable power in that part of the mind. They think these powers is sufficient evidence that they have entrepreneurial talent and make attempts to get results in such work, but they soon find that the inspiration in that direction does not last and they are compelled to try something else. They find that their commercial or venture abilities are not large enough to carry out their ambitions along this line. In consequence they turn their attention to the next venture that looks promising. There are thousands of minds who are constantly affected in this way, drifting from one action to another.

They imagine that because someone is succeeding in a certain work they may also succeed in that work, provided they have inclinations along that line. They also imagine that they are the very ones to enter every particular field where the demand for great service and great ability is required. The reason is their minds are controlled by appearances and what they feel as the result of switching of energy here and there from one ability to another. Such people therefore cannot rely upon the sense of feeling in any line of action because it is seldom normal.

To produce a normal sense of feeling for the purpose in question we should never pay any attention to what others have done or are doing because the success of others proves nothing as far as we are concerned. We must not look at the power of another man's brain, but try to find what there is in our own brains. We should never permit the enthusiasm of others to intoxicate our own minds. We should let others be enthused in their way and we should let them concentrate upon what work they like. But we should not imitate others either in thought, enthusiasm or feeling.

The course to pursue is to watch yourself closely for some weeks or months and try to discover in what ability you feel the most power. If you feel the greatest power in a certain ability and in that one only, you may choose that ability without further examination and give it all your force, energy, ambition and desire, realizing that the application of that ability will bring the greatest results that you could attain in your life. But if there are several other abilities that seem to be equally strong, wait and watch more closely until you finally discover the seat of the greatest power. When two or more seem to be equally strong, and continue thus under the most rigid self-examination, choose the one that you can use to the best advantage now, and turn all your power for attainment and achievement in that direction.

When there is prolonged uncertainty as to where the greatest amount of power is expressed try to increase the power of every part of your mind by directing the subconscious to express more power from within. The value of this is found in the fact that the greatest amount of power always goes to the largest ability so that an increase of power will in every case reveal the existence of the leading talent or faculty in your possession. After you have made the sense of feeling normal so that you can feel the state of your mind as it really is, you can always depend upon the law that whatever you feel that you can do you have the power to do. And you may proceed to act along that line knowing that you will succeed, no matter how difficult the undertaking may seem to be. It is the presence of great power in a certain ability that makes you feel that you can do things by using that ability. Therefore when you can feel what ability is the largest and strongest you know positively what you can do, what you can accomplish and what you should undertake. True, a great deal of training of that strongest faculty may be required, but since the talent, the ability, and the power are there the results must follow when the practical application is made.

Master Mind

In order that we may rise in the scale of life the mind must fix attention upon the ideal. And the ideal may be defined as that possible something that is above and beyond present realization. To become more and accomplish more we must transcend the lesser and enter the greater. But there can be no transcending action unless there is a higher goal toward which all the elements within us are moving; and there can be no higher goal unless there is a clear discernment of the ideal. The more distinctly the mind discerns the ideal, and the more frequently the ideal is brought directly before the actions of attention the more will the mind think of the ideal; and the mind invariably moves towards that which we think of the most. The man with no ideals will think constantly of that which is beneath the ideal, or rather that which is the opposite of the ideal; that is, he or she will think the most of that which is low, inferior and unworthy. In consequence he or she will drift more and more into the life of nothingness, emptiness, inferiority and want. One will steadily go down into the lesser until we start wanting more, both on the mental and physical platform.

The man, however, who has high ideals will think the most of the greater things in life, and accordingly will advance perpetually into the possession of everything that has greatness, superiority and high worth. The wise men of the past declared that the nation with no visions would perish. And the cause of this fact is simple; when we are not going up we are going down. To live is to be in action and there is no standstill in action. To continue to go down is to finally perish. Therefore to prevent such an end we must continue to go up. But we cannot continue to go up towards the higher unless we have constant visions of the higher. We cannot move mentally or physically towards that which we do not see. Nor can we desire that of which we have never been conscious.

In like manner the individual who has no ideals and no visions of greater things will continue to go down until life becomes mere emptiness. Thus everything in that person's nature that has worth will perish, and finally one will have nothing to live for. When one discovers himself or herself you will find that there are but two courses to pursue; to continue to live in the vale of tears one has made for themselves; or to ascend towards the heights of emancipation, those heights which can be reached only by following the great vision.

It is the visions of greater things that arouse the mind to greater action. It is higher ideals that inspire man to create more nobly in the real, and it is the touch of things sublime that awakens in human nature that beautiful something that makes life truly worth living. Without ideals no person will ever attain greatness, neither will there be any improvement in the world. But every person who has ideals, and who lives to realize his ideals, will positively attain greatness, and will positively improve everything, both in his life and in his environment.

It must be clearly evident to all minds who understand the true functions of the ideal that the life of man will be worthless unless inspired by the ideal, and also that everything that is worthwhile in human existence comes directly from man's effort to rise towards the ideal. Such people, therefore, who are constantly placing high ideals before the world in a manner that will attract the attention of the world; it is such individuals who invariably have the greatest mind of all. The majority have not the power to discern the ideal clearly without having their attention aroused by the vivid description of some lucid mind that already does see the ideal. But when their attention is aroused and the ideal is made clear to their minds, they will begin at once to rise in the scale. That individual, therefore, who is constantly placing high ideals before the minds of the many, is causing the many to rise towards the more worthy and the more beautiful in life. In consequence one is not only doing great things for oneself, but one is causing thousands of others to do great things. The individual is not only awakening the superior powers in his own nature, but he is also awakening those powers in the natures of vast multitudes.

However, to place ideals before the minds of others, it is not necessary to make that particular purpose a profession, nor is it sufficient to reveal idealism in the mere form of written or spoken words. Actions speak louder than words and the man who does things exercises a far greater power for good than the man who simply says things. The ideal can be made a vital and a ruling element in every vocation. And all men and women can reveal the ideal through their work without giving voice to a single word concerning any particular system of idealism. But it is not necessary to be silent concerning those sublime visions that daily appear before the mind, although it is well to remember that we always secure the best results when we do a great deal more than we say. The man who makes his work an inspiration to greater things will invariably do greater and greater work and he will also cause thousands of others to do greater work.

He will make his own ideals practical and tangible, and will thereby make the ideal intelligible to the majority. For though it is true that great words inspire the few, it requires great deeds to inspire the many. The man who makes their own life worthwhile will cause thousands of others to make their lives worthwhile. In consequence the value and happiness that one will add to the sum total of human existence cannot possibly be measured. He is placing great and living ideals before the world and must therefore be counted among those who possess the greatest mind in the world.

The man who performs a great work has achieved greatness, but his work is the work of one man only. That man, however, who places high ideals before the minds of the many, thereby awakening the greatness that is dormant within the many, causes a greater work to be performed by each one of the many; thus he gives origin to a thousand great deeds, where the former gives origin to a few only. That he is greater in exact proportion is therefore a fact that cannot be disputed. For this reason we must conclude that the master mind of all is invariably that mind that can inspire the greatest number to live, think and work for their vision.

To awaken the greatness that is dormant in man is to awaken the cause of everything that has real worth in the world. Such work, therefore, is the greatest of all great work and it is a work that lies within the power of everybody. For we all can awaken the greatness that is latent in other minds by placing high ideals before those minds. The great soul lives in the world of superior visions and aims to make those visions real by training all the powers of mind and personality to move towards those visions. And here it is highly important to realize that when the powers of mind and personality steadily move towards the ideal they will create the ideal more and more in the present, thereby making the ideal real in the present. To live where there is neither improvement nor advancement is to live a life that is utterly worthless. But improvement and advancement are not possible without ideals. We must have visions of the better before we can make things better. And before we can make things better we must discern the greater before we can rise out of the lesser. To advance is to move towards something that is beyond the present; but there can be no advancement until that something is discerned. And as everything that is beyond the present is ideal, the mind must necessarily have idealism before any advancement can possibly take place.

Everything that is added to the value of life has been produced because someone had ideals; because someone revealed those ideals; and because someone tried to make those ideals real. It is therefore evident that when lofty ideals are constantly placed before the mind of the whole world we may add immeasurably to the value of life, and in every manner conceivable. The same law through which we may increase that which is desired in life we may apply for the elimination of that which is not desired. And to remove what is not desired the secret is to press on towards the ideal. The ideal contains what is desired, and to enter that which is desired is to rise out of that which is not desired. Through the application of this law we eliminate the usual method of resistance, which is highly important, because when we antagonize the wrong or that which is not desired we give life to the wrong, thereby adding to its power. The fact is that we always give power to that which we resist or antagonize. In consequence we will, through such a method, either perpetuate the wrong or remove one wrong by placing another in its place. However, no wrong was ever corrected in the world until the race ignored that wrong and began to rise into the corresponding right. And to enter into this rising attitude is to become an idealist. It is not the iconoclast, but the idealist who reforms the world. And the greatest reformer is invariably that man whose conception of the ideal is so clear that his entire mind is illumined by a brilliant light of superior worlds. The thoughts, life, words, actions, in brief, everything connected with his existence gives the same vivid description of the ideal made real. Every person with whom one may come in contact will be inspired to live on those same superior heights of sublime existence.

When we try to force any ill away from any part of the system, be the system that of an individual, a community, or a race, we invariably cause a similar or modified ill to appear in some other part of that system. For the fact is that no ill can be eliminated until it is replaced by wholeness. Wholeness will not enter the system until the system enters wholeness. We must enter the light before we can receive or possess the light. And to enter wholeness is to enter the ideal and perfect existence.

To enter the ideal, however, it is necessary to understand the ideal. Every form of emancipation as well as every process of advancement will depend directly upon the mind's understanding of the ideal, and its aspiration towards the ideal. A strong ascending desire to realize the ideal will, in the life of any individual, cause the entire system of that individual to outgrow everything that is inferior or undesirable. In consequence complete emancipation and greater attainments must invariably follow.

When we understand this subject thoroughly we realize that if all the strong minds in the world could constantly face the ideal, giving all their power to the attainment of the ideal and living completely in the reality of the ideal, a live current permeating the whole race would begin to move towards the ideal. The natural result would be that the ideal would be realized more and more in every individual life of the race. This possibility demonstrates the extreme value of the ideal and the importance of living absolutely for the ideal. It also demonstrates the fact that all such men and women who are constantly placing the ideal before the minds of the world possess the greatest master minds in the world. It is only such minds that can inspire the masses of minds to discern the ideal, to desire the ideal, and to live for the realization of the ideal.

CPSIA information can be obtained at www.ICGtesting.com
Printed in the USA
BVOW08s0037280515

402193BV00010B/36/P

9 781438 228976